WITHDRAWN

Learn to Paint People
Quickly

Learn to Paint People
Quickly

Hazel Soan

BATSFORD

To the people who matter most in my life,
some of whom are pictured in this book.

First published in the United Kingdom in 2017 by
Batsford
1 Gower Street
London WC1E 6HD

An imprint of Pavilion Books Company Ltd

ISBN: 9781849943949

A CIP catalogue record for this book is available
from the British Library.

10 9 8 7 6 5 4 3 2 1

Reproduction by Tag, UK
Printed and bound by Leo Paper Products Ltd, China

This book can be ordered direct from the publisher
at the website:
www.pavilionbooks.com, or try your local bookshop.

TThe accompanying *Learn to Paint People Quickly* DVD from Hazel Soan is
available from the SAA, society for all artists, at www.saa.co.uk

Page 1: *Following Watercolour (51 x 51cm/20 x 20in)*

Page 2: *Feeling Free 1 Watercolour (25.5 x 30.5cm/10 x 12in)*

Acknowledgements

It was a privilege to write this book on one of my favourite subjects.
Thank you to my publishers, Pavilion, and especially to Tina Persaud
and Cathy Gosling, for making the book possible. Thank you to
my editor Lucy Smith for making the ride so enjoyable and to the
designers, Hannah Naughton and Gail Jones for doing such a good
job and bearing with my whims. Thank you to Rosie, my sister, for her
comments on the draft and to my husband for keeping quiet while I
was reading the layouts. Thank you to all the people who allowed me
to paint them, without whom this book could not exist. And thank you
to my readers for letting me know that these books encourage them,
it makes it all worthwhile.

Contents

Introduction

This book is all about the exciting and inspiring challenge of painting people, which is less complicated than you may expect. Within these pages you will discover how readily figures can be suggested on the paper or canvas so that you can include them in paintings in a convincing and lively manner. You will learn the value of proportion, pose and lighting; how clothing describes form and provides colour and pattern; and how a likeness is created. You may be surprised to find that spaces are as important as the figures themselves – and relieved to find that less is often more!

Packed into this book is all the practical stuff you need to know in order to paint people in a convincing way. It can be read in less than an hour, so hop on board and learn to paint people quickly!

▷ Rock Pools *Oil on board (25.5 x 30.5cm/10 x 12in)*

CHAPTER 1
Understanding the essentials

The importance of people in a painting

Have you noticed that when you place a figure or a face in a painting the viewer's attention is invariably drawn to it? And that if the figure is credible it brings life to the painting but if not, it is an irritant that cannot be ignored?

This attraction is natural with such subjective association. People bring meaning and narrative into paintings and as a result we are oddly annoyed by any misrepresentation of our own species. Consequently, the painting of people comes with rather more accountability than other subjects such as trees or buildings, and is either avoided altogether or accompanied by much anxiety. No wonder many aspiring artists find the idea of painting people scary!

△ Fallen Cowboy *Watercolour (38 x 56cm/ 15 x 22in)*
Painting is full of trial and error. Be like this cowboy – if it goes wrong, pick yourself up and start again! It may feel uncomfortable, but it isn't failure; it's learning.

▷ Lincoln in Sunshine *Watercolour (28 x 38cm/ 11 x 15in)*
The inclusion of people adds significantly more context to a composition. The figures in this street bring life to the painting.

From the painting's point of view

Children have no trouble depicting people – the angst only arrives when we try to imitate reality and portray likeness. The remedy is to approach representation from the painting's point of view and 'think like a painting'. Painting is two-dimensional and therefore concerned with the elements that pertain to the flat world. These elements are line, shape, pattern, colour, light and shade. The painter looks for descriptive lines, lively shapes, exciting patterns, captivating colours and agreeable tones. With these components the three-dimensional world is brought to life by implication on the flat surface.

Children paint people and faces without fear. Their figures are symbolic, using descriptive features. They do not worry about literal likeness because they are not yet concerned with suggesting the third dimension in their picture.

Santa Monica Beach Basketball *Watercolour (23 x 30.5cm/9 x 12in)*

From this detail you can see that the watercolour is made up of dabs, blobs and brushstrokes, yet they are laid in a fashion that presents the viewer with no problem in believing they represent a group of people playing basketball.

Dabs, blobs and brushstrokes

On the flat surface of the painting the image is made up from a series of dabs, blobs and brushstrokes in a variety of shapes and colours, orchestrated to represent an image from the three-dimensional world. To the paper or canvas, therefore, people are no different in principle from trees, flowers or rocks: all are represented by arrangements of various marks.

Entertaining the eye

Like other forms of art, painting is initially entertainment as far as the audience is concerned. If it entertains the eye we delve in deeper and find the messages for our soul. The paper or canvas represents the stage, the painted brushstrokes words and music. Once you grasp that a figure or a face in a painting is in reality a bunch of colourful marks put together in an artful and visually entertaining way, the fear of painting people will simply fall away. Painting people need not be scary at all – in fact it is really fun.

△ Each to His Own Trajectory *(detail)*
In this detail it is clear to see that paintings are made with a variety of colourful shapes and marks. Only when you see the whole painting, shown opposite, do they transform into figures crisscrossing Liverpool Street Station.

▷ Each to His Own Trajectory
Mixed media on canvas *(91 x 122cm/36 x 48in)*
The more people you put in a painting, the less they have to be identifiably people as each figure in a crowd carries the others along. So be brave – the more people you paint, the easier they will become.

CHAPTER 2
Proportions

Getting the proportions right

Very little is needed to persuade the viewer that a person has been represented in a painting – just a small oval blob above a couple of upright lines or an elongated triangle can do the trick. However, making the figure appear credible and at home in the painting requires a few basic 'keys'. The first key is proportion.

Proportion is the relationship of one thing to another in terms of size or shape. Painting a figure in proportion means getting the head, limbs and torso in the right relationship. Thanks to our familiarity with the subject, the proportions need only be mildly convincing for a figure to be believable.

The artist Ian King offers an easy way to portray a suited standing figure: blend the two letters M & W together!

An oval dot over a few vertical brushstrokes is all that is needed to suggest jaunty figures.

▷ Bro Code *Watercolour (76 x 102cm/30 x 40in)*
When figures are painted in proportion they are not only convincing but informative. Here the size and length of heads, arms, legs and bodies communicate an image of youthful camaraderie.

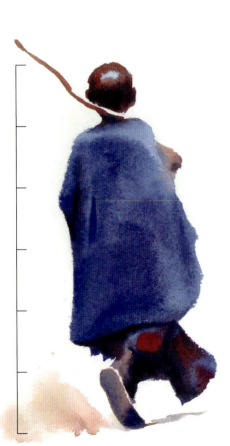

African Apprentice *Watercolour (25.5 x 35.5cm/10 x 14in)*
Here the boy's head goes into his height about six times. His head is rounder than that of the adult opposite and the proportion of his head to body will decrease as he grows.

Heads up: head to body proportion

The size of the head in relation to the length of the body is the first consideration. In an adult the head is oval and fits into the total length of the body seven or eight times, depending on height. In children the head is rounder and larger in proportion to body height, which means that if you paint adult figures with heads too big or too round they will look more like children.

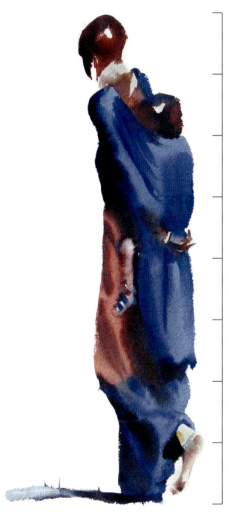

Madonna Blue *Watercolour (56 x 25.5cm/22 x 10in)*
The Maasai tribe are a tall people. The mother's head fits into her body eight times, so from the proportion of her head to her body we can judge that this woman is indeed tall.

The body, arms and legs

The proportions of the limbs in relation to each other and the torso may seem obvious, but it is easy to misrepresent them in the flush of painting. Some guidelines to bear in mind: legs are longer than arms and both bend at halfway points (the knees and elbows); hands reach down to the mid-thigh and meet at the groin; arms usually fold above the waist; and the width of outstretched arms approximates to a person's height. Getting these interrelationships roughly in proportion will help you to create convincing figures.

▷ The arms extend to the thigh in a standing figure.

△ The arms bend and fold across the body above or at waist level, depending on the pose.

◁ Hands meet across the body at groin height. People typically take up this pose when waiting in a queue or posing for a photograph.

△ You can paint convincing distant figures in watercolour by blending the colours wet into wet: indicate the head and limbs first, add in the body while the paint is still damp and let all components blend together.

△ Arms and legs bend roughly in half, at elbow and knee, which means the upper and lower part of the limbs are approximately the same length.

◁ A child's limbs are proportionately shorter in length. Avoid painting children too small in relation to adults – it is estimated that a child reaches half their adult height by the age of two.

Face: the facts

The human face has a set of relative proportions that are easily implied. Unless the person is in close-up you need only indicate these relationships sketchily to create convincing faces on your figures. The shadows cast by the features are often more useful for suggesting the face than the features themselves. Likeness to a specific person requires more particular positioning of the features and is covered more fully in the chapter on portraits (see page 98).

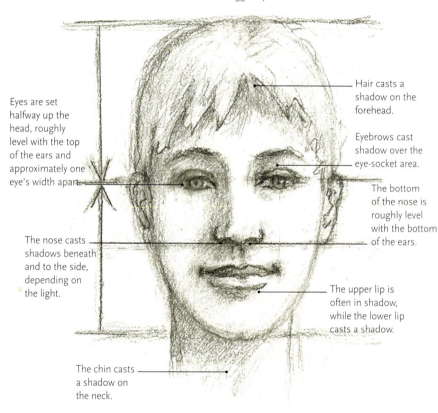

The adult head is not round but oval and egg-shaped.

Hair casts a shadow on the forehead.

Eyebrows cast shadow over the eye-socket area.

Eyes are set halfway up the head, roughly level with the top of the ears and approximately one eye's width apart.

The bottom of the nose is roughly level with the bottom of the ears.

The nose casts shadows beneath and to the side, depending on the light.

The upper lip is often in shadow, while the lower lip casts a shadow.

The chin casts a shadow on the neck.

Sketching profiles and three-quarter views on the train and in queues soon makes faces familiar territory.

Shadows adequately suggest facial features if the eyes, nose, mouth, ears and hairline are presented in correct proportion to each other.

Symmetry

For a figure to be convincing, the right and left sides must be in similar proportion. It is easy to forget to address this simple and obvious relationship when concentrating on other parts of the body, so a loose initial sketch encompassing the whole figure is often advisable to check everything is at least roughly in proportion before proceeding with paint or detail.

The Mexican *Pencil sketch and watercolour (38 x 18cm/15 x 7in)*
Here the man's body is painted quite loosely but the proportions are still maintained and correlate right and left: the legs and arms bend at the halfway mark, and the elbows, knees and feet run parallel with the tilt of the head and shoulders.

When right and left limbs present different configurations, check that your rendering of the bent limb would straighten out to roughly the same length as the straight limb. By applying basic proportions to this figure, the left and right sides are kept in the correct relationships: the straight arm extends to the thigh, while the right arm bends at waist level, with upper and lower arm equal in length. The left leg bends level with the knee of the right one.

Strolling the Strand *Quink ink (30.5 x 25.5cm/12 x 10in)*
When more than one figure is involved, ensure that they relate to each other. The man here is taller than the woman but they are both painted in the same relative proportion. Note where the toes and feet touch the ground: these levels must match in order for the figures to link.

Perspective

Proportion in relation to other people or features in the foreground or background of a painting needs to be taken into account for the space depicted between them to appear feasible. Here the rules of perspective come into action and enable the painter to show figures in convincing relationship with each other.

The use of perspective implies distance by means of a reduction in scale towards the horizon: people nearby are painted larger in scale than people in the background. The horizon is always at eye level, so whether you stand or sit to paint determines whether your figures 'shrink' in scale from the feet up, from the head down or in both directions. Here are some examples.

Passage in Time
Oil on board
(15 x 30.5cm/6 x 12in)
Standing to paint: the heads of the figures are at my eye level, so, in accordance with the rules of perspective, the heads remain level with mine as they move further away and the figures 'shrink' upward.

△ The Pulse of Africa *Acrylic on canvas (58.5 x 89cm/23 x 35in)*
Sitting to paint, my eye level is at chest height. Following the
rules of perspective, the chests of the students remain level with
the horizon, while the heads at the back of the line move down
the picture plane towards the horizon and the feet move up, so
'shrinking' the figures in both directions.

◁ Standing out from the Crowd *Watercolour (76 x 102/30 x 40in)*
Looking down on the figures: the horizon (my eye level) is above
the top of the painting and very little distance is implied in the
picture, so the figures shrink far less dramatically in scale than
in the other examples.

Foreshortening

Perspective also comes into play within the form of the figure, causing foreshortening whenever a part of the body juts into the foreground or recedes into the background. The distance is short – maximum 2m (6½ft) – but the results of foreshortening can be unnerving to paint because normal proportions appear all messed up. An obvious example is someone lying feet first towards you.

Measuring foreshortened proportions
Hold a pencil vertically at arm's length in front of you (yes, the classic artist's pose) and use it as a measuring rod to compare different parts of the body, for example the size of the head to the foot, the thigh to the calf. Keep the pencil in an upright plane, as if pressed against a windowpane.

Chilled *Watercolour (56 x 76cm/22 x 30in)*
At this angle, the feet become large in relation to the head: measure the length of the boy's left foot with your thumb and you will see that astonishingly it is the same length on the picture plane as the distance from the top of his head to his waist.

CHAPTER 3
The pose

Plausible poses

Portraying figures in natural and lively poses is a must if you want them to look credible in the painting. An active posture is generally more interesting than a static pose, and offers a storyline. The aim is to present poses that are anatomically possible and circumstantially probable. Happily, as with proportions, poses do not have to be highly accurate to be effective.

A pose needs to appear balanced, which means checking where the weight is placed. The balance can be assessed and adjusted with the use of an imaginary plumb line dropped from the nape of the neck to the feet.

If a figure is standing straight with the weight evenly distributed, the line touches down between both feet. When the weight is taken by one foot or the other, the ankle taking the weight lies directly below the nape of the neck.

Pillars of Society
Watercolour (35.5 x 28cm/14 x 11in)
The men here are all standing still but there is variety in their poses: from left, the first man's weight is mainly taken by the back foot, the man in the middle balances evenly between both feet and the man on the right leans all his weight on the right foot.

△ A vertical line dropped from the nape of the neck shows that the weight in this pose is distributed evenly between both feet.

▷ When the figure leans, his weight is taken by one leg. An imaginary plumb line from the nape of neck meets the ankle taking the weight.

In a Hurry *Acrylic on canvas (18 x 13cm/7 x 5in each)*

While walking the men transfer their weight from one foot to the other, so the balance changes within the stride.

Indicating the movement

Simply by painting one foot higher than the other, you can suggest a person is walking towards or away from the viewer. The foot taking the weight falls directly below the nape of the neck.

From the side view, the triangular gap made between the legs is indicative of where the person is in their stride. A big triangle is made between the legs when the stride is fully extended, while a small triangle is made below the knees when the back leg is bent at the knee (shown below right).

◁ We can tell the figures are not static but walking towards us because one foot is shown higher than the other.

Mile Jedinak, Crystal Palace at Home
Watercolour 15 x 15cm/6 x 6in)
When the figure is in swift motion, the centre of gravity may be
in front or behind the figure, with the body leaning forward or
backwards into the pose and often using the arms for balance.
Drop a line down from the nape of the neck and you can see the
centre of gravity is behind the deft feet of the footballer.

In the Surf *Oil on canvas (30.5 x 35.5cm/12 x 14in)*
To suggest rapid movement use blur and ambiguity in the
brushwork. The angle, the looseness of the poses and the
accompanying splash clearly communicate figures in action.

Sitting and leaning

When weight is taken by something other than the person – a wall, chair, or table – the pose is dependent on the support. The task is to show the connection between figure and prop in order to convince the viewer that the person is linked inextricably to the prop and cannot hold the pose without it.

Sitting and leaning poses come with benefits – the prop can be usefully employed to obscure 'difficult' parts of the body, such as hands.

Lunchbreak
Watercolour (35.5 x 20cm/14 x 8in)
Very little actual information is given here, but it is enough to suggest two seated figures enjoying a conversation.

Conversations in a Courtyard *Watercolour (25.5 x 35.5cm/10 x 14in)*
In this painting the women are connected to the table and objects by means of small warm shadows.

The Journal

Oil on canvas (28 x 46cm/ 11 x 18in)
The girl is sitting on the bed, supported by her elbow and hip. The soft folds of the counterpane obscure some detail and show that her body is supported but also sinking into the bed.

Proximity shadows

Where the figure meets and touches the support, deeper shadow is cast. This is called a proximity shadow, and it is very useful because it establishes a point in the painting where you can show the viewer that two surfaces meet and interact. Think of the prop as a continuation of the figure, rather than a separate item, and you will imply this sense of mutual belonging.

The proximity shadow is a place where light is blocked and may therefore be the darkest point in a painting.

Beach Girls *Watercolour (25.5 x 25.5cm/10 x 10in)*
Darker tone in the long blue shadows cast across the ground denotes the proximity shadows where the girls' bodies make contact with the sand. The angle of the shadows serves to describe the flatness of the support on which the girls sit.

Making contact

Proximity shadows are not only important where contact occurs with props or supports but also where contact occurs between people and other surfaces, or within the figure itself. The connection point is shown in the painting by a proximity shadow. Quantum physicists explain that we never really touch things – our atoms literally float in very close proximity to each other. Seen this way, the proximity shadow signifies this space in between.

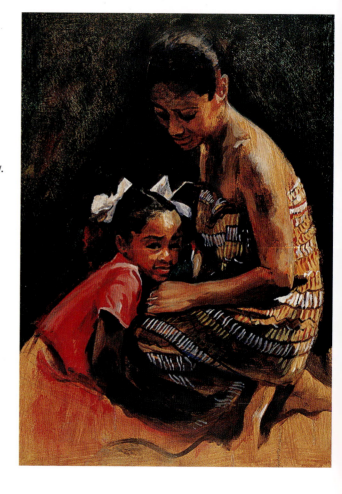

Be my Shelter *Acrylic on paper (76 x 56/30 x 22in)*
Lines of shadow in the painting demarcate the points where the mother and daughter touch and where the mother's arm meets the sarong.

Gaps and spaces

In a painting, figures do not need to be touching for a connection to occur. On the picture plane the spaces between figures are as vital to the pose, stance and composition as the figures themselves. Getting spacing 'right' between people and things is key in order to link them. Go through the pictures in this book and instead of looking at the figures, study the spaces between them and the gaps visible between limbs and body. In artspeak these areas are called negative spaces, and they should be factored into the composition.

Boys will be Boys *(Detail)*
Oil on canvas (35.5 x 46cm/ 14 x 18in)
The gaps between legs, arms and bodies and the spaces between the boys not only define the poses but have the power to affirm the friendship between them.

Negative shapes are made by the spaces
around and between solid things.

The shapes in between

The shapes of negative space are called negative
shapes. Although intangible in the three-dimensional
world, on the two-dimensional painted surface these
shapes are very real and as important to paint as the
brushstrokes that depict the solid forms. Negative
shapes help to describe the person's pose from
the outside and enable the artist to determine the
contour line around the body. Within poses, bent
limbs often create negative shapes that are triangular
in character, for example between an arm on the
waist and the torso or between striding legs.

Everything is Black and White
Acrylic on canvas (76 x 102cm/30 x 40in)
This painting was inspired by the spaces in between silhouetted
travellers waiting in a dazzle of morning light at a bus stop in
Valletta. I painted the white negative shapes instead of the figures.

CHAPTER 4
Lighting

Light and shade

There is one more vital ingredient to add to proportion and pose before the figure can fully inhabit the painting. This is light, or rather light and shade. Light emanates from a single source, such as the sun, the sky or a lamp, or from multiple sources, such as streetlights or combined interior lighting. The direction and angle from which the light comes and its strength are crucial considerations for an artist, because creating interesting counterchanges between light and shade is the substance of representational painting.

△ The three ingredients that are important to making a lively, convincing figure are clear in this watercolour sketch: the woman is in proportion, her pose looks plausible and the light and shade on her clothing offer a lively and descriptive pattern.

▷ The Portal, Kairouan *Watercolour (28 x 38cm/11 x 15in)*
In this painting we can believe sunlight is shining on a Tunisian market scene from a top-right direction because the figures, ramparts, stalls, etc., with their lighter sides facing to the right of the picture plane, are all shown lit from the same source.

Tone

The gradations between light and shade are collectively termed tones or values, and three-dimensional form is implied on the painted surface by their interrelationship and counterchange – darker against lighter and lighter against darker. Confusion in seeing and painting tonal variation often causes weakness or mismatch in paintings, especially if the light indicated on the figures does not marry with the light implied in the rest of the painting. Tonal values are always relative and only have to be convincing in terms of the painting, rather than a replica of their strength in real life or photographs.

To enhance contrast, show a lit feature against a darker background (here the face) and a shaded feature (back of the neck) against a lighter background. Think of phrases such as 'darker than' or 'lighter than' to determine the strength of individual tones in relation to each other.

The Light of Collioure
Watercolour (25.5 x 25.5cm/10 x 10in)
Three main tones are needed to imply the
three dimensions – light, dark and mid
tone. Here the sunlight on the figures is the
light tone, the shadows under the tables
and awnings are the dark tone, and the
background is mid tone.

Sean & Yassen
Oil on board (28 x 35.5cm/11 x 14in)
The shimmer of white water is the lightest
tone in this painting; the silhouettes of the
boy, his dog and the rocks are the darkest
tones, while the swathe of beach is the
mid tone.

Light sources

As the earth moves around the sun there is a change in the direction and angle of light, which alters tones and colours. The sun reaches its highest point in the middle of the day, after which light and shade 'swap places'. A painting will not make sense to the viewer if it appears to display multiple angles of light. Once the direction is determined, stay consistent. The following pages demonstrate the effects of light from different angles.

A sunlit scene begins the day lit from the east, by late morning front-lit, at midday top-lit, during the afternoon side-lit from the west, and by evening back-lit.

Liquid Lines *Oil on canvas (51 x 25.5cm/20 x 10in)*
The girl is in full overhead light. Her head casts the long shadow over her torso and light gleams on the front of her limbs, pushing shadow out to the sides to be represented simply as a contour line against the water.

Top lighting

In the middle of the day, and under overcast skies, light comes from overhead. This top light manifests itself in slivers of light on upward-facing features. The tops of heads, shoulders and folded arms, the lap of a seated figure, the instep of a foot and a bent-over back are all areas where lighter tonal values will be displayed on a figure lit from above.

▷ Against a dark background, the highlights from a top light stand out vividly.

▷ ▷ Sarong *Watercolour (51 x 28cm/ 20 x 11in)*
In equatorial regions the noonday sun is directly overhead. The light catches the top of this woman's head and highlights the sarong at the base of her back and on her calf as she walks.

Front lighting

While this angle works well in photography, light mainly from the front is not easy pickings for a painter, especially in watercolour. The features are clearly visible but there is little useful tonal variation playing over the surface to suggest the third dimension. With few shadows evident in full light the painting can appear flat. Shadows made by folds in clothing or from projecting features are precious under this light source.

△ The background, the shadows created by the creases in the sleeves and the cast shadow under the arm enable this front-lit jazz musician to come alive on paper.

◁ In watercolour a figure lit from the front is created with the surrounding background. Here a space left in the background allows this front-lit figure to emerge. Placing the man's shadow to the left helps root him to the ground.

Three-quarter lighting

When a figure is lit mostly from the front, but with enough shade on one side to make modelling possible, the light and shade create an attractive asymmetrical exchange of tones across the body and three-dimensional form is easy to imply.

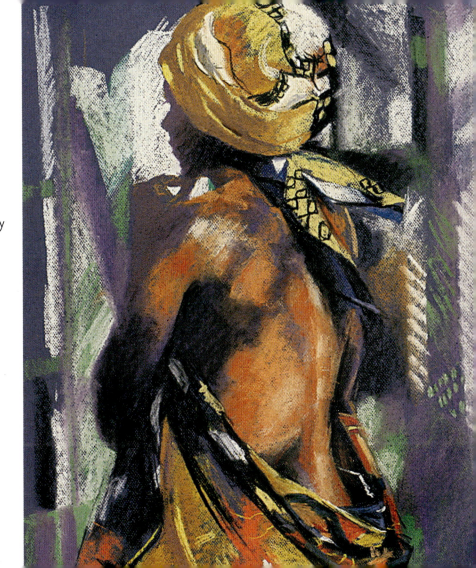

Fabric of Africa
Pastel (91 x 61cm/36 x 24in)
Here the figure is three-quarter lit from the right-hand side and flecked with dappled shadow. Most of the picture is in a cheerful high key created by the light on the yellow fabric, which is contrasted with violet shadow.

Side lighting

With this angle of light, one half of the figure is bathed in light and the other half is in shadow, offering a pleasing balance of tonal interchange on the painted surface. Side lighting is fun to paint, as both the right and left side are often entertainingly broken up by zigzag patterns of alternating light and shadow from folds in clothing. For maximum effect, contrast the darker, shadier side of the figure against a background lighter in tone and place the lighter side of the figure adjacent to darker tone.

◁ Light from the side creates delightful zigzag patterns of light and shade from the folds and creases in fabric.

▷ In Anticipation
Oil on canvas (76 x 76cm/30 x 30in)

▽ This is My Town
Watercolour (43 x 56cm/17 x 22in)

Creating a perfect balance of
light and shade, sidelight makes for
strong compositions, as you can see
from the black-and-white versions of
these two paintings.

Quarter lighting

An interesting counterchange in light and shade is set up when a figure is lit by light coming from above and behind. Under this quarter-lit angle the figure is predominantly suffused in shade with just a splash of light on one side. Set amid darker tones, the glimpses of light appear more vivid and create exciting tonal counterchange.

Large Glass II
Watercolour (76 x 102cm/30 x 40in)
In this watercolour the light is coming from the left above and beyond the figures. The lit features are made visible only where they come up against a darker tone, and are imagined in the 'missing' pieces of a head or limb.

Back lighting

A figure is thrown into silhouette by backlighting. This light, known in visual art as contre-jour (meaning 'against the day'), creates dramatic contrast between light and shade. Dark figures become flat shapes since there is no modelling. Mid- or dark-tone backgrounds bring out exciting halos of light around heads, and rims of light balance on shoulders or slither down sides that catch the light.

◁ Taking the Weight *Watercolour (33 x 30.5cm/13 x 12in)*
Exiting the dark interior of the stable, the cowboy is thrown into silhouette against the bright light outside. Carrying his riding paraphernalia, he makes a rugged and fascinating shape.

▷ Streetlight *Watercolour (28 x 38cm/11 x 15in)*
The sunlight shining down the street creates backlighting for the figures, casting them into silhouette. Against the mid and dark tones of the buildings, the sunlight catching on the top of heads and shoulders is left as untouched white paper to show the dazzling effect of the light.

Demonstration: Back lighting

Back lighting is a compelling angle of light and the contrast of tones makes for a strong compositional pattern. Here the canvas is stained with Raw Umber to create a warm mid tone and the darkest and lightest tones are painted in with a brush and palette knife. Working in this way allows a painting to come together quickly.

Colours
Burnt Sienna
Cadmium Red
Raw Umber
Ultramarine Blue
Titanium White
Yellow Ochre

Stage 1: I laid out the composition on the stained canvas, paying attention to individual proportion and perspective. Before progressing any further, I checked the walking poses for balance and plausibility.

Stage 2:
I painted the silhouettes with blacks mixed from Ultramarine Blue and Raw Umber/Burnt Sienna, applying them with a flat brush and palette knife, diminishing the depth of tone with distance.

Stage 3: I mixed Titanium White with Yellow Ochre and, with a palette knife, laid the paint between the black shapes to create a dazzling light. Darker tone on the right emphasizes the brightness.

Stage 4: Next I mixed Cadmium Red into the faces and hands, providing links with the colour of the buses in the background. Creamy white paint brings out the halos of light around the heads and shoulders.

The Spaces Between Us *Acrylic on canvas (46 x 61cm/18 x 24in)*

Final Stage: The lighting, the proportions and the poses have all contributed to this vibrant exchange between light and dark, which treats the shapes of light between people as equal to the figures in terms of importance.

CHAPTER 5
Clothing

The advantage of colour

One of the benefits of figure subjects is the bright colour that often comes with clothing. Fabrics dyed in vivid hues and vibrant patterns provide generous colour for painting. In addition, the folds and creases set up exciting tonal exchanges and the drape of clothing can hint at the form of the figure beneath. These things entertain the eye and can be used to great advantage in a painting.

△ The Elders *Watercolour (30.5 x 66cm/12 x 26in)*
The cloaks may conceal the figures of the Maasai within their folds, but the way they drape suggests the form of the individual beneath.

▷ Framed by Dust *Oil on canvas 51 x 51cm/20 x 20in*
The red and blue colours of the Maasai man's cloak and sarong are the crux of this painting and the movement of the robe establishes the breeze alluded to by the drifting dust.

Dressing the figure

Clothing can be used to add a striking accent of colour or create an adept tonal exchange. The splash of a red shirt amid a sea of green or a white suit against a dark background, for example, are excellent compositional devices. The joy of dressing figures is that you can change the outfit to suit the needs of your composition – there is no need for veracity here. Your subject may be sporting a beige shirt but if red is needed to bring the painting alive, red it becomes!

Red is a striking colour in a painting. Both of these compositions are painted with the same set of colours and benefit noticeably from the introduction of the red clothing.

Crossing St Mark's Square
Oil on canvas (76 x 91/30 x 36in)

Café Society
Oil on canvas (152 x 152/60 x 60in)

The marriage of colour and tone

Colour matters but tone is still king. Bright colours will stand out like sore thumbs if the key is too high. When colours are fully lit they will be vibrant, bright and obvious, but colour in shadow is more muted. To ensure your colouring retains the right tone, paint a dark undertone first and then add the colour. In watercolour you can drop the colour into the undertone while the paint is still wet to create a more radiant effect.

Rock-solid Friendship *Watercolour (15 x 35.5cm/6 x 14in)*
The boys are in silhouette but still exhibit some colour in their clothing against the pale shoreline.

(Detail)
To maintain the dark tone of the heads and bodies, Light Red, Cadmium Red and Cerulean Blue, which are opaque colours, were dropped into the damp first layer of Prussian Blue.

Blending, blur and separation

While clothing is enjoyable to paint, it can become overcomplicated by details, patterns and folds. The best way to find the information that matters to the painting is to observe the subject through half-closed eyes; you will find that the meaningful tones remain distinct while the minor variants vanish.

Colours lose distinction when a figure is in motion. By blurring detail and encouraging ambiguity, you can impart a sense of energy and movement to the figure. Paradoxically, lessening definition usually makes clothing appear more life-like than showing every detail. In general, aim for definition in the lighter mid tones and softening in the shadows.

▷ The man's red jacket and dark trousers blend completely together in the shade covering his back.

▷ ▷ In these backlit figures the definition between different colours and the keen difference in tone between faces and clothing is softened by blending.

◁ On the lit side of these figures crisp delineation is shown between the top and bottom parts of clothing, while on the shaded side they blend.

▷ Bronco
Watercolour (20 x 20cm/8 x 8in)
Movement is implied in the figure by blurring the face and clothing beneath the cowboy's hat with splodges and splashes, as if the rider is coming in and out of focus.

Folds and creases

There is no doubt that folds and creases in fabric are two of the chief delights of painting clothes. The reason is simple: they create patterns of alternating light and shade, and this tonal variation is very satisfying to behold and to paint.

△ Listening to the Wind
Oil on canvas (122 x 76cm/48 x 30in)

▷ Saffron Robes
Watercolour (25.5 x 18cm/10 x 7in)
The wet-into-wet technique of watercolour makes representing folds a quick process. I painted the robe with pale orange and then, along the line of the fold shadows, added more concentrated pigment into the damp wash. The paint spread out gently, creating effortless gradations in tone.

▷ Balanced View
Oil on canvas (20 x 20cm/8 x 8in)
In this oil painting it is light rather than shadow that is added to show folds. I painted the darker, shaded colour of the sarong first and then added the highlights on the ridge of the folds with paler paint.

Patterns and logos

Unless it is the detail of a pattern that excites you, pattern may seem like too much intricacy to manage. However, patterns do bring richness and texture to a painting and are fun to paint. The secret lies in 'less is more'. You do not have to imitate the pattern – including a fragment is enough for the viewer to imagine the existence of much more. Just place a dab here, a touch there, to show some of the arrangement, ensuring that the pattern follows the folding of the fabric so that it plays its part in creating form. Let it lose itself in the shadow, be revealed in the mid tones and fade in the light. The same applies to logos – limit your marks to mere suggestions and the viewer's eye will fill in the rest.

The logo on the back of the anorak aligns with the swing of the pose. It is only loosely suggested but has substance in the sketch.

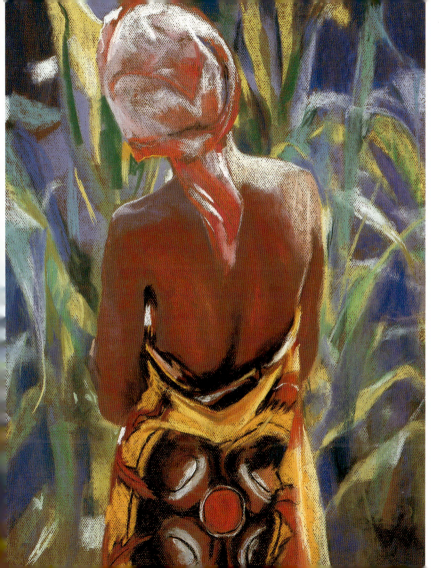

The Maize is Ripe, Juarati
Pastel (76 x 56cm/30 x 22in)
Pattern appears to dominate this pastel painting, but look more closely and you will see just how little detail is actually shown. The important thing is that it follows the creases and folds in a believable fashion.

Using stripes

Striped fabric is really useful to the artist. With just an indication of direction, stripes can deftly describe the form of a limb or torso and the angle of a pose. Like pattern, stripes are subservient to the rolling folds and creases. Allow them to get lost and found in the undulating landscape of the fabric.

◁ The mere indication of pink stripes on the cowboy's shirt is enough to describe the form and position of the arms and body and allows the rest of the figure to be rendered loosely to enhance the sense of action.

A few stripes are enough to show their general width and direction. There is no need to show every stripe – too much information will stifle liveliness.

◁ Learning the Ropes *Watercolour (56 x 76cm/22 x 30in)*

Accessories

Giving a figure something to hold adds interest to the shape and gives narrative to the pose. Bags, umbrellas, books and so forth are helpful accessories, so take advantage of them whenever you can.

The addition of the stick adds a story to the old man's pose.

Hats are useful because the brim and crown catch the light and the shadow cast by the brim obscures facial features.

Umbrellas bring colour and tonal contrast. They are lit on top and cast shade underneath.

The brim of a hat and the white pages of an upturned book provide vibrant lights against darker backgrounds.

Though not accessories in the literal sense, animals and children are useful additions to extend the profile of a figure in a painting.

Bags introduce colour and interest (and avoid the necessity to paint the hands!)

Demonstration: Clothing

A race day where everyone had to wear blue and white inspired this painting. I stained the canvas with a blue undertone to give the blues greater depth and set out to create a sense of celebration and luxury.

Stage 1: Using dilute Raw Umber, I drew the figure leaning on the rail, glass in hand. The Umber and Ultramarine Blue act as an undertone for the shadows.

Stage 2: I indicated the folds with darker shadow within the general washes of blocked-in colour and used the same dark mix to delineate the strands of hair.

Stage 3: Next I added the mid tones – first the pale cool blues, made with Cerulean Blue and Titanium White.

Colours
Alizarin Crimson
Burnt Sienna
Cerulean Blue
Raw Umber
Titanium White
Ultramarine Blue
Yellow Ochre

The Blue Dress
Oil on canvas (76 x 56cm/30 x 22in)
Final Stage:
With a few tonal adjustments to the background and the back of the dress the celebratory atmosphere was achieved, so I decided the painting was finished.

Stage 4: Then I put in the deeper mid tones of both the cool turquoise and the warmer French Ultramarine.

CHAPTER 6

Figures in a setting

Figures in the landscape

This chapter looks at placing figures in settings in a lively, meaningful and accomplished way. Although the figures may be fairly small within the whole composition, and detail limited, it is crucial to keep in mind proportion, pose, lighting and colouring.

▷ **Passage of Time**
Watercolour (20 x 28cm/8 x 11in)
In this watercolour the figures, being darker than their background, could be painted on top to provide meaning and narrative to a simple setting.

Beneath Snoqualmie Falls
Watercolour (25.5 x 28cm/10 x 11in)
The figures here provide the scale that shows the height of the waterfall. As the sunlit bodies are paler than the background pool, I sketched them in pencil first to guide the wash of green around them.

The inclusion of people in landscapes provides a reference to the scale and proportion of the scene and offers a storyline. So it is preferable to plan the position of the people in the composition from the start rather than add them as an afterthought, especially in watercolour if the figures are lighter in tone than their background. In oils and acrylics and other opaque media, figures can be repositioned, added, or removed at will.

Cloak of Many Colours *Oil on canvas (25.5 x 51cm/10 x 20in)*
Oils are often painted from dark to light. The boy is picked out from the dark background with the light colour of the dusty ground, and his striped cloak is made colourful with opaque reds and blues. The distance implied between him and his cattle is conveyed by the diminishing scale and lighter tones.

Street life

Manmade landscapes benefit hugely from the inclusion of people: streets come alive when they are populated and comparison reinforces the scale of buildings. The more figures you include in the scene the less you have to worry about the definition of each one, so there is definitely safety in numbers! Place dark figures against lighter backgrounds and vice versa. Be aware of perspective and the correlation in diminishing size between the figures and the buildings, cars and other things.

In these paintings a crowd is readily understood, be it of commuters, traders or shoppers, even though little definition is offered in the sparsely indicated distant figures.

Suits *Oil on canvas (35.5 x 46cm/14 x 18in)*

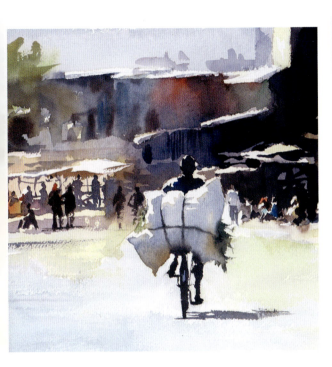

Pedal Power *Watercolour (20 x 20cm/8 x 8in)*

Retail Therapy, Oxford Street *Oil on canvas (122 x 91cm/48 x 36in)*

Café scenes

Figures in cafés and restaurants make popular painting subjects. Not only do they provide interactive sitting and standing poses but the tops of tables are often lit and the chair legs beneath are in shadow, offering the painter both variety of stance and lively exchanges between light and shade.

In these details you can see how the looseness of the brushmarks makes the figures appear lively, whether they are seated or serving at tables.

Al Fresco
Watercolour (25.5 x 35.5cm/10 x 14in)
With only a few colours the semblance of a busy street café is created with blobs and brushstrokes in a range of tones, from untouched white paper highlights through mid tones to the dark undersides of tables and chairs.

At the beach

Some of the best figure-painting opportunities can be found at the beach, as people relax into poses unencumbered by heavy clothing. The presence of a figure brings paintings of wide-open or empty shorelines instantly to life.

All you need is a few well-placed brushstrokes to indicate people in action and give a storyline to a simple scene, as can be seen in these three watercolours painted by the sea.

A Day at the Beach
Oil on canvas (25.5 x 51cm/10 x 20in)
Lit by sunshine, the variety of poses, bright colours and array of
accessories at the beach translate well into painting material.

Demonstration: An interior scene

A restored diner on Route 66 provides a perfect setting for a painting inspired by Edward Hopper. The bright light outside casts the diner into warm, dark shadow and highlights the solitary woman in the window.

Colours

Burnt Umber
Cadmium Red
Light Red
Ultramarine Blue
Yellow Ochre

Stage 1: After mapping out the composition with a pale Yellow Ochre and Ultramarine Blue undertone, I deepened the shadowed interior with a more concentrated Yellow Ochre and Burnt Umber wash.

Stage 2: The criss cross of the window frames and the pattern of light and shade on the figure complete the tonal pattern of the composition.

Stage 3 (Detail): I strengthened the skin tones in shadow with concentrated Light Red. The limbs are blended with the bench cushions while darker proximity shadows show where the body makes contact.

Stage 4: The introduction of the mid-tone buildings seen through the window helps to bring out the main focus, which is the light on the figure, and introduces warmth.

Diner *Watercolour (30.5 x 41cm/12 x 16in)*
Final Stage: I strengthened all the shadows with Burnt Umber and a little Ultramarine Blue to enhance the light on the woman by greater contrast of tone. The chequerboard tile lines complete the picture.

CHAPTER 7
Portraits

Catching a likeness

When the intention is to represent a particular person, the painting is called a portrait. Catching a recognizable likeness and character requires careful observation, especially of the face. Faces are not flat and features cannot just be pasted into position; the eyes, nose, mouth, chin, eyebrows and hairline must be seen in relation to each other and integrated to construct the whole form of the head. The distances and spaces between facial features are just as important as the features themselves.

Philippe *Ink and watercolour (28 x 35.5cm/11 x 14in)* Portraiture requires study. Here the left-hand picture was my first attempt and while it works as a face it does not look like Philippe. On the right is the second attempt, where I paid more attention to the shape of his face, eyes and eyebrows, and thus found his likeness.

Skin tones and colouring

To help sculpt the head, position your sitter so that more light falls on one side of the face than the other. Use warm colours such as Burnt Sienna, Brown Madder and Crimson for skin tones glowing with warmth. For the facial features that project – nose, mouth, cheeks and ears – use warm colours to bring them forward. Cooler colours, such as blues and greens, help to sink back the side planes and lower face.

Dark accents, such as the lip line, nostrils, corners of the mouth and eyes and the inner ear, can be shown warm and dark with deep crimsons and violets.

△ Val *Watercolour (51 x 30.5cm/20 x 12in)*
In this quick watercolour portrait, warm and cool colours of Yellow Ochre, Burnt Sienna and Prussian Blue are used in the skin tones while crimson and violet mark the nostrils, eyelid and inner ear.

◁ Juarati *Acrylic on paper (25.5 x 18cm/10 x 7in)*
Portraits can catch a likeness without being too explicit or literal. Here the colouring is limited to red, white, blue and black and the face is half obscured by shadow.

The eyes

Start work on the facial details by putting in the eyes. They are set back in the face, under the shadow of the brow. Paint the curve of the upper lid of one eye first, then bring in the iris and pupil, leaving a highlight in the eye. Next paint the shadow of the socket and the fold of skin above the eye and then lightly mark in the lower lid. Go across the bridge of the nose and mark up the other eye in the same way. Once established, the eyes become a measure and guide for the other features.

Points to note: the upper eyelid overlaps the top of the iris; the bottom of the iris sits on the lower lid; the top lid is darker than the lower lid; the inside lid gets lost as it merges with the socket cavity next to the nose. Crimson is used here for the darks.

The distance between the eyes is approximately the width of an eye. The second eye here is on the lighter side of the face so, though the shapes may be similar, the treatment is not a repeat of the first eye.

The nose

To measure the length of the nose, compare it with the width of the eyes. From the front, the nose is created with shadow and highlight; only as it turns toward the profile does its outline become distinct. The nostrils point towards each other and can be painted quite dark, set softly in the shadow under the tip of the nose, which is usually the lightest part.

△ A difference between the amount of light and shade on each side of the face makes it easier to use tone to sculpt the shape of the nose.

▷ In this three-quarter view, the line of the nose becomes more apparent.

The mouth

It is easier to paint the mouth closed, with a relaxed expression. The lips follow a curve and are rounded, not flat. Begin with the contour line between the lips for both positioning and expression – tilting up the corners hints at a smile – then add the upper and lower lips. The form of the mouth is created with light and shade.

Mark the line where the two lips meet and end the corners of the mouth in soft indented shadows beneath the cheeks.

Shape the top lip, which is usually shaded, and will be darker on the non-lit side.

Shape the rounded lower lip, lighter in tone than the upper lip. The cleft above the lips is indented – the dip can be shown with light and shade.

◁ To establish the exact position of the corners of the mouth, drop imaginary lines down from the middle of each eye.

The hair

The hair should look as if it belongs to the head, not added like a wig. While it consists of myriad fine strands, overall the hair is three-dimensional. Rather than paint individual hairs, look for sections, main clusters of strands, overlaps and the shadows between. Show where hair and face meet in a 'lost and found' fashion, varying between lights and darks and hard and soft edges: in some places there will be no contrast, in others the contrast will be stark. Half-close your eyes to limit yourself to the important lights and darks.

Rather than overcrowd the hair with a lot of detail to show this complex plaited style, the main contrasts of light and shade build the form.

Even though the girl's hair colour is much darker than her skin tone, the connection is not abrupt. The hair is darkest where it meets highlit parts of the face and transitions gently in shadow.

Demonstration: Portrait of Ulene

In order to focus, do not fret about catching a likeness. Instead, concentrate on rendering lines, shapes, light and shadow by measuring and comparing as carefully as possible, then a likeness should result by default. Stop, step back from your work and check it against your sitter. Resist the temptation to correct or tidy up the portrait unnecessarily. When you catch the likeness it may register as a visual jolt or a moment of recognition

Colours

Alizarin Crimson   Sepia
Burnt Sienna   Ultramarine Blue
Permanent Rose   Violet
Sap Green   Yellow Ochre

Stage 1: Over a pencil drawing and pale Yellow Ochre undertone, I began detail with the eyes, using Alizarin Crimson to mark in the eyelids and Sepia for the iris.

Stage 2: I used Burnt Sienna as the primary skin tone, building to a darker tone on the shadier side of the face. Then I introduced more warmth with Alizarin Crimson.

Stage 3: I painted the upper and lower lips with Alizarin Crimson, paying close attention to the change of tone from side to side and on top and bottom lip.

Stage 4: The next step was to introduce the vibrant colours and deep tones of the hair and T-shirt wet-in-wet, with concentrated colour added into dilute washes. I mixed Ultramarine Blue and Sepia for the black of the hair and used Permanent Rose neat for the shirt.

Ulene Watercolour (51 x 41cm/20 x 16in)
Final Stage: I brushed a pale blue wash gently over the shaded side of the head, neck and shirt and deepened the eye sockets. As I evened out the pink on the lower lip the 'hello' moment happened and I knew I had caught Ulene's likeness.

CHAPTER 8
Go for it

Painting people is fun

Painting people is an exciting challenge, and you are obviously up for it because you have reached the end of the book! The three main things to remember are proportion, pose and lighting. There is no need to describe every detail – instead, leave something for the viewer to imagine. Practice is everything: the more people you paint the more confident you will become. Congratulate yourself proudly when you succeed, forgive yourself quickly if you fail. Soon you will be painting figures and faces in an accomplished and convincing manner so they look and feel at home in your paintings.

To Our Shadows We Belong *Oil on canvas (81 x 152cm/32 x 60in)*
Be unpredictable. The strength of this painting lies in its avoidance of repetition, despite a similar theme across the picture plane: the poses, head heights and clothing combinations all differ. Throughout, tone is still king, to ensure the harmony of the whole.

Index